Happy Birthday
Marilyn 1997

Loretta & Norm
Rombach

*Dedicated to the "angels" in my life, Glenda, Adrienne, Lara Elizabeth & John*

# Songs the Angels Sing

by Kenn Hayes

Printed in Hong Kong.
6  5  4  3  2  1     9 8  97  96  95  94

Publishers Cataloging in Publication Data.
Hayes, Kenneth B.  1940-
*Songs The Angels Sing* / Kenn Hayes.
          Poetry, Ballads and Music for Angel Lovers.
Summary: Song lyrics and poetry about angels.

ISBN 1-885514-001-8 (cassette & book package)     UPC No. 7 94214 0001 4

*"What know we*
*of the Blest above*
*But that they sing,*
*and that they love"*
WILLIAM WORDSWORTH

*Believing in angels is easy. We need only to think through the events in our lives when help came to us, help that was hard to understand or that we couldn't explain, and simply think of angels. Could it be? Is it possible that "Somebody up there really loves us" and that angels play a part in how that love is shown?*

*I hope that you enjoy this collection of pictures, songs, poetry and music and that it will help you with your own appreciation of the heavenly beings...the angels.*

## FLYING DREAMS

Tomorrow in the morning light
We'll awaken from tonight
But now that nightime's in the sky
with stars and moon and lullabies
Let's put on our angel wings and fly.

High above the city lights
Flying through starlit tonights
Away to angel land we'll fly
with quiet whispers you and I
To all our daydreams say goodbye.

Let's put on our flying dreams
and take the light from the moonbeams
On angel wings we'll go tonight
we will fly while sleeping tight.

*Blow a kiss across the Milky Way*
*and say goodnight to this today*
*Let's blow a kiss to stars and sky*
*and sing our angel lullaby.*

Tomorrow in the bright sunlight
We'll soon forget about our flight
But now we'll kiss the moon and sky
and sing an angel lullaby
And thank our dreams we can fly.

Let's put on our flying dream
and take the light from the moonbeams
On angel wings we'll skyward soar
we will fly to Heaven's door.

## CAROUSEL ANGELS

Carousel angels and gold shiny rings
Wishes delicious and magical things
Bright crystal candles aglow from a star
Angels are watching it all from afar.

Mythical gardens and fountains of youth
Things made of fancy
and things needing proof
Narwhals of silver, a unicorn spoof
Angels are watching it all from our roof.

Carousel angels and gold shiny rings
Baby is sleeping as mother now sings
Our lullaby angels still watch and keep
Guarding our sweet dreams
while we are asleep.

Rings of pure diamond, a thin jasper thread
Sweet Gypsy beauty, the Prince she will wed
Glamorous visions will dance in your head
Angels are watching it all from your bed.

Alice's wonder, tin man and sweet tarts
Fantasy island and dinosaur art
Dreams, dreaming and dreamland
that all play a part
Angels are watching it all from your heart.

Carousel angels and gold shiny rings
Baby is sleeping as mother now sings
Our lullaby angels still watch and keep
Guarding our sweet dreams
while we are asleep.

# EVERY TIME A BELL RINGS

Standing, waiting
Work to do
Angel wings when we are through
Bells are ringing
Happy times
Angel wings and nursery rhymes.

Every time you hear them tolling
Every time you hear them ring
Think of lullabies sweet angel
And know that he has got his wings.

Heaven's laughing
all is well
Angel wings brought by the bell
Bells keep ringing
Angels sing
Lullabies and angel things.

Every time you hear them ringing
Every time you hear them toll
Think of lullabies sweet angel
And their wings of solid gold.

Angel wings
and lullabies
Sleepy baby, don't you cry
Standing, waiting
Work to do
Angel wings when we are through.

13

## UNIFORMS OF SNOW

Ten thousand little angels
Lined up from star to star
Did you ever stop to wonder
How many there really are?

How many angels are there
Does anybody know
Do they really get all dressed up
In uniforms of snow?

Angels dressed in white
In uniforms of snow
How many angels are there
Does anybody know?

It's all one grand procession
From heaven down to earth
Some carry a golden trumpet
For heralding a birth.

Row after row of angels
A Milky Way of lights
How many angels are there
To light the starry nights?

Angels dressed in white
In uniforms of snow
How many angels are there
Does anybody know?

Angels dressed in white
In uniforms of snow
How many angels are there
Does anybody know?

## ANGELS CALLING FROM THE THRONE

Angels calling from the throne
Of gold inlay and emerald stone
From crystal floors and brilliant sea
Their heavenly voices calling me
Their heavenly voices calling me.

Messengers from heaven above
Poised to call with heaven's love
With their celestial symmetry
Herald angelic poetry
Herald angelic poetry.

Angels in a tumultuous whirl
Precious stones and gates of pearl
Calling mortals home to be
Sanctified by Heaven's Three
Sanctified by Heaven's Three.

## ANGELS UNAWARES

So who's to know . . .
Who loves you so
The angels as they come and go.

So who's to kiss . . .
Whose love is bliss
The angels come to tell us this.

 The angels always seem to know
 The angels help us as we go
 Sometimes we are so unaware

So who's my love...
It's from above
The angels come as mourning doves.

So who's to care . . .
Whose love is fair
The angels as we're unaware.

The angels always seem to know
The angels help us as we go
Sometimes we are so unaware

The angels always seem to know
The angels help us as we go
Sometimes we are so unaware

The angels always come and go
The angels help us here below
Sometimes we are so unaware
Sleep sound my love, His angels care.

## ANGEL SHADOWS

Angel shadows on my closet
Angel shadows on my bed
Angel shadows in my memories
Angel memories in my head.

Those sweet souls, the angels' shadows
Pressing nearer to our side
Angels here to guard us
With gentle helpings, they glide.

Angel shadows here to watch us
Angel shadows here to see
Angel shadows here for guarding
Angel shadows just for me.

Those sweet souls, the angels' shadows
Pressing nearer to our side
Angels here to guard us
Even though sometimes we hide.

Angel shadows on my closet
Angel shadows on my bed
Angel shadows in my memories
Angel memories in my head.

## SWEET MELODIES

Angels in the sky
Flying very high
Look and you will see
There for you and me

Angels all around
Up high or on the ground
Watching as we sleep
Tucked under our sheets

*Singing angel lullabies*
*Melodies that harmonize*
*Symphonies of angel lullabies*

Angels in the sky
Ask the angels why
Watch and you will hear
Angels at your ear

Angel voices sing
Sweet melodies they bring
Singing us to sleep
Our souls love will keep

*Singing angel lullabies*
*Harmonies that mesmorize*
*Symphonies of angel songs tonight*

Angels in the sky
Ask the angels why
Watch and you will hear
Angels at your ear

*Celestial sleepy symphonies*
*An orchestra on starlit seas*
*Singing sweet angel melodies*

*"How did he git thar? Angels.*
*He could never have walked in that storm*
*They just scooped down and toted him*
*To whar it was safe and warm*
*And I think that saving a little child,*
*And fotching him to his own,*
*Is a derned sight better business*
*Than loafing around the Throne."*

JOHN HAY
*Little Breeches*

## ANGELS MUST' A GIT HIM THAR

The storm, she was a blowin'
And Johnny, he was a goin'
But the wind,
she was a mite too much fer him.

The angels, they ain't loafing
They're always watching over you
'Cause thar might be things
you just can't git through.

The angels scooped down and took him
To whar it was safe and warm
And they tucked him into bed,
 until the morn
Yup, they tucked him into bed,
all safe and warm.

*How did he git thar? Angels.*
*He could never have walked in that storm*
*They just scooped down and toted him*
*To whar it was safe and warm.*

When the storm, she is a blowin'
And you don't know whar you're goin'
We hope them angels
ain't loafing 'round the Throne.

The angels scooped down and took him
To whar it was safe and warm
And they tucked him into bed,
 until the morn
Yup, they tucked him into bed,
safe and warm.

25

## GOOD NIGHT SWEET PRINCE

Good night, sweet prince good night
Now let the angels sing in flight
Good night, my princess too
A lullaby that sings good night to you.

Good night
Good night

Good night, sweet prince good night
Now rest your noble heart and head
Good night, my princess dear
Asleep you go before the day appears.

Good night
Good night

Good night, sweet prince
Now let the angels sing in flight
Good night, my princess too
A lullaby that sings good night to you.

Good night
Good night
Good night
Good night

Good night
Good night
Good night
Good night

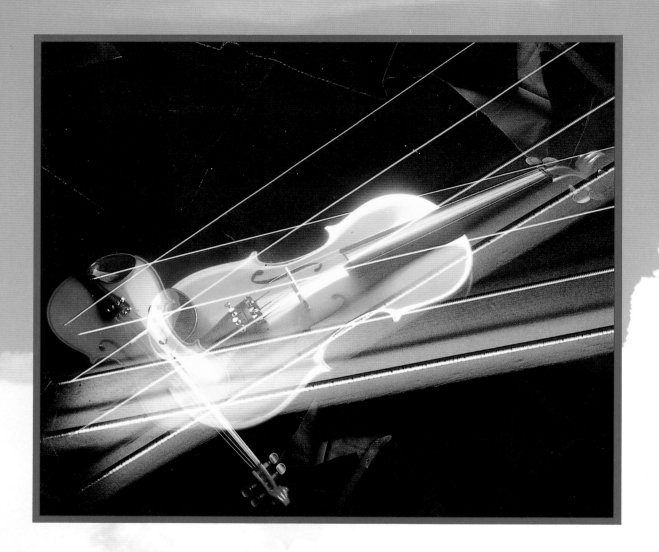

*Credits:*

The Book *"Songs The Angels Sing"*
By Kenn Hayes
Concept by Denise Buzy-Pucheu and Kenn Hayes
Cover design & Typography by Paul Perlow, Paul Perlow Design
Photography by Mark Archer  (pgs 5, 10, 12, 18, 20, 22)
& Wayne Armstrong  (pgs 8, 14, 16, 24, 26, 28)
Special thanks to the following writers and poets for their contributions:
Saint Paul the Apostle, Cowper,
Emily Dickinson, John Hay, John Milton,
William Shakespeare, R.H. Stoddard,
Harriet Beecher Stowe, William Wordsworth,
...and of course Clarence.

The Music *"Songs The Angels Sing"*
Produced by Randy Rigby
Lyrics by Kenn Hayes (except, "Sweet Melodies" which was co-authored by Ed Edwards)
Music by Randy Rigby (except, "Every Time A Bell Rings" and "Sweet Melodies" by Ed Edwards)
Arrangements by Randy Rigby, Ed Edwards and Don Garberg
Lead Vocals by Sheri Cory, Kenny Andrus & Mark Oblinger
Background Vocals by Mark Oblinger, Sheri Cory & Ed Edwards
Piano and Keyboards by Don Garberg
Guitars by Randy Rigby & Ed Edwards  Bass by Mel Brown & Jim Fletcher
Drums & Percussion by Steve Ivey
Recorded and mixed by John Macy at Kerr/Macy Studios in Denver, Colorado

Thanks for your help,
Sara, Aaron & Ellen Archer.  Bridget Carroll, Charles Adler & The Grisley's.
Shirley Gurtler, Elich Gardens & Norm's Dollhouse
Tyler and Ben Chandler, Tammy Freund and Ann Corinao.

Thanks to Jon Chandler for all the good ideas.

A special thank you to my old friend Terry Johnson,
without whose help and support this project would still be up in the clouds.